PREFACE TO BC

KEYS

The editors can see no justification for re to key C, with a gradual addition of other follows:—

1) The chief cause of hesitation and inaccuracy has nothing to do with key: it is due to uncertainty as to the pitch of the notes to be sung. A fluent application of the solfa syllables to the staff does away with this difficulty. Therefore, what is needed is a grading of this application in a manner suitable for all keys. That is what this Series sets out to supply.

2) C is not the easiest key in either the treble or the bass stave. (It is the easiest key for the piano, certainly, but the mental processes of sight-singing, especially in the earliest years, are totally different from those involved in playing a keyboard instrument.)

3) Although early results may be quicker if key C is adhered to at first, succeeding stages are rendered more difficult; ultimately, the most fluent reading is secured by variety of keys from the beginning.

4) So long as there are no accidentals (which do not come until a much later stage), pitch names are only an encumbrance to the mind and a hindrance to reading. All that matters at first is to know the position of doh, and to be ready with the most commonly used leaps; for instance: to remember that if d is on a line, d m s and s t r¹ will be line, line, line, and f l d¹ will be space, space, space; that if d is in a space d m s and s t r¹ will be space, space, space, and f l d¹ will be line, line, line. The less the pianoforte keyboard is thought about the better.

KEY SIGNATURES

There is no need for beginners to know the full meaning of key signatures. The following two simple rules are all that is necessary:

1) Where there are sharps at the beginning of the line, the last sharp, that furthest to the right, is t; d¹ is a step above.

2) Where there are flats at the beginning of the line, the last flat, that furthest to the right, is f; d is three steps down, f m r d.

Pitch names need not be thought of at all. But, in order to meet the needs both of teachers who use key signatures from the beginning and those who do not, in the first 50 tunes the key signature is given, and the position of d is also indicated by ⊗. From No. 51 the ⊗ is omitted.

Practice should precede theory; knowledge of unessential details should be left over until progress justifies their introduction.

PRELIMINARY SOLFA TRAINING

It is assumed that preliminary solfa training has been sound, and that the three cardinal chords of the major key are thoroughly familiar. To attempt to apply solfa names to the staff without thorough and systematic modulator practice previously is to court disaster. Reading to laa is usually mere guess-work. No certainty can be obtained without a constant use of the solfa syllables. If a good foundation of solfa has been laid most easy leaps are prepared for. Reading from solfa notation also is an invaluable and necessary aid to securing fluency in the use of the syllables. Material for this will be found in Books XI and XII, which contain solfa notation only: they are intended to be preparatory and complementary to the staff books.

GRADING.

No collection of sight-singing examples can possibly meet all needs, or suit everybody's plan of grading. To secure sufficient variety, and to maintain interest in class, it is necessary to employ various forms of reading practice by use of the modulator, written examples and printed tests. Teachers should be ready to invent, and write on the board, additional melodies giving practice in any special difficulties of either time or tune which may arise in a lesson. It must not be assumed that every tune in these books is necessarily more difficult than those immediately preceding it. Excepting for the new factor, the first tunes in each Section are sometimes easier than those at the end of the previous Section. But the Sections are arranged in order of difficulty and the tunes graded within each Section.

With tune, the primary difficulty is to attain speed in thinking out the solfa names of the notes, but facility in this is merely a matter of careful grading and well-directed practice. Progressions commonly in use should be systematically introduced and practice limited to those until they are mastered.

The plan of grading in this book is one which can be adapted to meet various needs according to the ideas of the teacher concerned.

The tunes are arranged in three Sections.

Section 1 is limited to the use of the doh chord with its various leaps, and scale passages.

Section 2 adds the use of the soh chord; and

Section 3 the fah chord; but in the case of the soh and fah chords leaps are limited to thirds only, so that throughout the book the only leaps greater than a third are those of the doh chord.

Each Section is subdivided into three parts, A, B and C.

In each case:

    A is limited to tunes containing only ♩ ♩ ♩· ♪.

    B introduces rests, but none shorter than a whole pulse.

    C introduces ♫ but always stepwise in itself and in quittance.

Within these limitations ♫ is not difficult, and the increased rhythmic interest which it affords is too valuable a factor to justify its postponement longer than is necessary. Teachers who prefer to omit it until the three cardinal chords have been learnt can do this by leaving out the C groups until all the A and B tunes have been studied.

SUGGESTED PLANS FOR READING

In the early stages of reading it is suggested that each tune may be sung in all of the following ways:

    1) To solfa without time.
    2) In monotone (*a*) to time names, (*b*) to doh.
    3) Combined time and tune to solfa.
    4) Combined time and tune to laa, twice if necessary, and then once at least with all expression marks observed (and to an accompaniment where the teacher is sufficiently skilled to improvise one).

The class should always beat time or tap each beat silently. It is desirable to use tapping in the early stages but to proceed to beating as soon as the class is ready.

When the class is sufficiently advanced each test should be sung at least three times, as follows:

    1) To solfa.
    2) To laa.
    3) With all expression marks observed (and to an accompaniment where the teacher is sufficiently skilled to improvise one).

After the earliest stages of note-to-note reading, classes must learn to think in phrases. As an aid to this, phrasing is marked in all tunes, and cases of irregular rhythmic structure are noted. Observation of these points of construction not only helps towards more intelligent reading but also increases the interest of the lesson. All repeats should be observed: expression marks in brackets refer to the second time.

Tempo and other indications may or may not be attended to on a first reading according to the capacity of the singers, but at a later stage all indications should be observed in order that sight-singing may be linked up with musical enjoyment. There is too often a tendency to divorce sight-singing from music, and one object of this collection is to provide material which is at once musical and useful, and which will help towards making this part of the singing lesson a delight to the class.

To add interest, the nationalities of the tunes are given. Very slight alterations have been made occasionally in order to bring tunes within the limitations of a particular section; all such cases are indicated by a *.

The proportion of tunes containing certain leaps, e.g., d¹-m and others, is not the result of an arbitrary choice but of an analysis of many hundreds of simple folk-tunes.

This analysis has revealed that much sight-singing that has been based upon theoretical plans is not in line with the findings resultant upon the arranging of a large number of folk-tunes in order of difficulty. It may be argued, therefore, that the basis of the scheme followed in these books is a natural and not an artificial one. The collection thus becomes a compendium of the difficulties likely to be met with in elementary reading.

INDEX

SECTION 1. NOS. 1—59

1A. Nos. 1—33. Doh chord with all its leaps, and scale passages. Time values: ♩ ♪ 𝅗𝅥 ♩· 𝅝

1B. Nos. 34—42. As 1A, plus rests, but with none shorter than a whole pulse.

1C. Nos. 43—59. As 1B, plus ♫ stepwise in itself and in quittance.

SECTION 2. NOS. 60—80

The *soh chord* is added but with leaps of a third only; i.e. s–t; t–s; t–r¹; r¹–t.

2A. Nos. 60—68. Time values: ♩ 𝅗𝅥 ♩· 𝅝 .

2B. Nos. 69—72. As 2A, plus rests, but none shorter than a whole pulse.

2C. Nos. 73—80. As 2B, plus ♫ stepwise in itself and in quittance.

SECTION 3. NOS. 81—110

The *fah chord* is added but with leaps of a third only; i.e., f–l; l–f; l–d¹; d¹–l.

3A. Nos. 81—99. Time values: ♩ 𝅗𝅥 ♩· 𝅝 .

3B. Nos. 100—104. As 3A plus rests, but none shorter than a whole pulse.

3C. Nos. 105—110. As 3B, plus ♫ stepwise in itself and in quittance.

Section IA. Nos. 1-33. Doh chord (with all its leaps) and scale passages.

2

SECTION IB. Nos. 34-42

As Section I A, plus rests (none shorter than whole pulse).

SECTION II. Nos. 60-80

The *soh chord* is added but with leaps of a 3rd only, i.e. s-t, t-s, t-r', r'-t.
Section IIA. Nos. 60-68. Leaps of a 3rd in the soh chord (no rests or pp).

60 Moderato — French*

61 Allegro giocoso — German*

62 Allegro — German

63 Andante (Five phrases each of two bars) — German

64 Moderato — French

Waltz time — German

71

p — *cresc.* — *dim.* — *p* — *cresc.* — *f* — *dim.* — *p*

Allegretto (Three phrases, each of 4 bars) — French

72

p — *dim.* — *pp*

SECTION IIc. Nos. 73–80

As above, plus ♩♩ stepwise in itself and in quittance.

Lively — British

73

mf — *p* — *pp cresc.* — *mf* — *dim.* — *p*

Moderato — Dutch

74

f — *p*

Moderato (4 phrases each of 2 bars, followed by 3 of 2) — German

75

mf — *p* — *cresc.* — *mf*

SECTION III. Nos. 81–110

The *fah chord* is added but with leaps of a 3rd only, i.e. f-l, l-f, l-d', d'-l.
__Section IIIa Nos. 81-99.__ Leaps of a 3rd in the fah chord (no rests or ♪♪).

As IIIA, plus rests (none less than whole pulse)

SECTION IIIc. Nos. 105-110

As above, plus _pp_ stepwise in itself and in quittance.

OXFORD UNIVERSITY PRESS